MW00910738

Honey *on* Hot Bread

and Other Heartfelt Wishes

by Joni Hilton

Cover Design: Deanna Walker
Book Design: Ryan Knowlton

Published by Covenant Communications, Inc.
American Fork, Utah

To Bob, Richie, Brandon, Cassidy, and Nicole

Other books by Joni Hilton:

As the Ward Turns
Around the Ward in 80 Days
Scrambled Home Evenings
Dating: No Guts, No Glory
Guilt-Free Motherhood
That's What Friends Are For

*T*his book is for you. It contains the love, the hopes, and the dreams I have for you, because you are a very special part of my life. It can lift, comfort, and inspire you through whatever life brings your way—whether you are young, old, or somewhere in between. I offer these wishes as precious blessings to ponder daily, and to study for the timeless advice within them.

These pages also contain my own innermost feelings and wishes, because the only true gift is a gift of self. Cherish this book. Keep it as an heirloom, adding your own feelings as you journey through life. Most of all, know always that it is given with love.

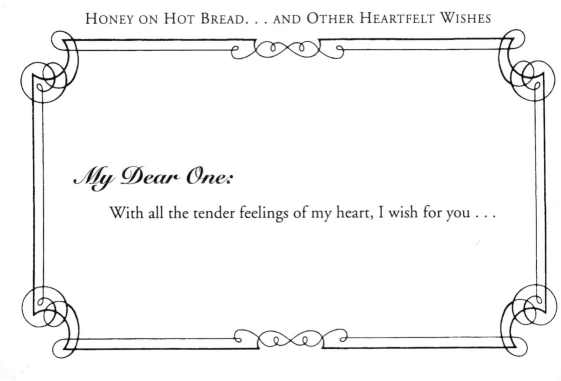

My Dear One:

With all the tender feelings of my heart, I wish for you . . .

Breathtaking Moments: Times when you catch your breath and marvel at what lies before you. It might be a scarlet sunset or a perfect, pink rose. Take a moment to appreciate the magic of everyday events—baby chicks emerging from their shells, hurried people holding doors for one another, snowflakes fluttering silently to blanket barren trees. It could be kites, balloons, or wishing stars. The world is filled with wonder. It's all there if you look.

Imagination: A mind free to wonder, "What if?" Stay as creative as a child, for all youngsters start life as creative little geniuses. Take delight in your thoughts, even the silly ones (perhaps especially the silly ones). Your mind is an amazing machine. It can crank out one marvelous idea after another. Don't let anybody turn it off.

Curiosity. Thirst for knowledge, Dear One. Be the one who asks the most questions. Look underneath, behind, inside. Experiment and challenge. Be intrigued; look for great lessons in small things. The greatest thinkers have always been fascinated by that which others overlook.

A Love of Learning. May books be your constant companions, and may each new fact you learn spark interest in learning another. May you be brimming with enthusiasm for the adventure of gaining knowledge, and may the world unfold its magnificent lessons to your eager mind. May you continue to be a scholar who never stops discovering.

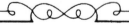

Humility. In your joyous travels through life, may you remember that no matter how much you learn, there is always much, much more you do not know. Remain teachable, and allow yourself to be receptive to the wisdom of the ages.

Great Thoughts. May your quiet moments of reflection be not so much about day-to-day events, or worries that will vanish in a year, but thoughts that elevate your spirit, thoughts that lead to action and improvement. May your focus extend to the poor, the unhappy, the less fortunate of our world. Free yourself from trivial concerns, and discover solutions that make the world a better place.

One Perfect Day. May your dreams come true at least once (if not several times!). Whether your fantasy includes walking through a sunlit forest, sailing on a deep blue ocean, or lying in a meadow of wildflowers, I hope you'll have one perfect, sparkling day when everything goes exactly as you'd like.

A Love of Nature. May you appreciate all that grows, and find it fascinating every time you see a butterfly, knowing that it started as a caterpillar. May the stars and moon enchant you; may the mountains and oceans overwhelm you with their splendor. And may the softest summer breeze carry your heart, like a feather, on its wings.

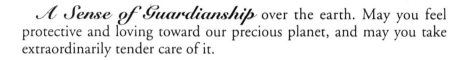

A Sense of Guardianship over the earth. May you feel protective and loving toward our precious planet, and may you take extraordinarily tender care of it.

A Clean World in which to live and flourish. Like every other being on the earth, your lungs draw in air that has swirled about our planet for centuries. Your body depends upon this world for food that is nourishing, healthful, life-giving. I wish for you a world of caring people to help you keep the world healthy and beautiful.

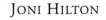

Safety. May your lifetime be one of freedom to walk, talk, work, and play without fear. May nothing ever harm you, my Dear One. May you live in peace, serene and strong, and feel protected while you sleep.

The Opportunity to Travel. May you have the pleasure of broadening your perspective by seeing other parts of this fascinating world. There is so much to learn from other places, other people, and other ways of life. And when you've gathered your experiences, I hope you'll cherish your own little corner of the world even more than ever before.

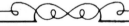

Self-Esteem. I'd give this one to you if I could, but you must earn it yourself (that's why it's called *self*-esteem). This much I can tell you: You can find it through serving others. Wait until you discover how wonderful you really are! (And if you have already made this wondrous discovery, you know how sweet its fruits can be.)

A Sense of Proportion. May you achieve excellence in many pursuits, rather than superiority in one. Do not become so narrowly focused in one field that you neglect the whole. You will be much happier if you are well-rounded and feel competent and skilled in many areas. Strive for balance in things mental, social, emotional, spiritual, and physical.

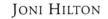

Persistence. Everyone is born with many talents, but talent alone will not bloom. If you have persistence, you will discover and develop your talents. Whatever your age or circumstance in life, relish the growth that comes through practice and discipline.

Self-Motivation. May you be a self-starter who never needs a prize dangled before you to get you going. May the satisfaction of a thing well done be your incentive. (Intrinsic rewards are always the best ones.) And may you be sought out by teachers, employers, and friends because you are brimming with inner drive and determination.

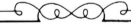

Freedom from the Need for Recognition. If you achieve goals for your own satisfaction, your accomplishments will be far greater than if you tailor your efforts to gain the applause of others. Nobody ever won a race by looking over their shoulder for someone else's approval.

Enthusiasm for Challenges. May you tackle problems with an eager, competitive mind, full of bold assurance and determination to conquer the difficult. When you meet obstacles—from learning a new skill to dealing with life's major dilemmas—may you see them as exciting mysteries to solve, opportunities to learn. Do not settle for less than victory.

Love of Truth. A lie is any effort to deceive, and it robs its teller of all peace. Discovered, it betrays trust and ruins friendships. Be honest in all your dealings, and you will possess great peace of mind, a calm heart, and the confidence that conquers fear.

Integrity. Cling to an ethical, moral sense that makes your actions match the highest principles you know. Do the right thing— even if no one else will ever know. When you tell the truth to others, that's honesty. When you tell the truth to yourself, that's integrity.

Belief in Your Worth. Know that you are a good person, born of good stock. Your veins flow with noble blood, a rich heritage of golden hearts and loving actions. Despite any mistakes you might make along life's path, know that you have, deep down, a choice and honorable soul.

Purity. Avoid all that defiles and corrupts. Keep your thoughts, language, and actions free from the grime of the world. Live a higher law, resisting the shadows of indiscretion, preferring the light of truth and dignity.

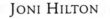

Influence for Good. Be a leader of the best kind: One who inspires the best in others. May you understand the incredible difference one good person can make. By following your example, may others forever improve their lives.

Strength of Character. Never apologize or be ashamed of your standards. Don't try to please a crowd; such groups have never been known for their wisdom or good taste. Follow your own star with unwavering determination, and you will become one of the Great Ones.

Music. Know and understand its power. Let its beauty inspire you to great heights, and bring you the rest of a gentle lullaby. Seek the best you can find, and surround yourself with tunes and instruments that lift your soul. If you sing or play music, may it bring great pleasure and stimulate you to seek its mastery.

Great Art. May you someday stand before a painting, your eyes filled with tears, as you suddenly realize that your soul has joined the artist's, and you marvel at the images captured on the canvas before you. Take time to appreciate the most excellent, the very finest.

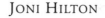

The Wind in Your Hair. May you find a way to run, to dance, to twirl through the air until it circles you like a parent's arms—gently, but securely. May you close your eyes and relish the moment, taking in the fragrances of blossoms far away.

A Love of Language. A whole culture, an entire library of literature, and every beating heart of a nation can be understood once you learn its language. May foreign words become familiar, and may understanding of other peoples flow easily into your mind. May you recognize and love the clever turn of phrase, and may you be blessed with many of your own.

The Joy of Pretending. May you thrill at the fun—and enlightenment—of portraying characters far different from yourself. And may your dramas always teach you, bringing you greater understanding of others. May you appreciate the theatre, and every fine performance.

Poetry. Not only do I hope you love and appreciate poems for themselves, but may you recognize poetry in the world around you. There is poetry in the squeeze of a hand, a scarlet autumn leaf, a majestic soaring eagle, and a flag against the sky. Most especially, there is poetry in a newborn babe.

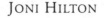

Abundant Love. You have my love forever, Dear One, simply because you *are*. May your cup also be filled from many sources. May love warm your soul when you are discouraged, and wrap its comforting arms about you when you are afraid. May others come to know and love you for the person you are, and may they show you, again and again, how much they care.

An Affectionate Nature. Love others despite their faults, with no strings attached. Extend your love through acts of kindness, gentle words, and ready hugs. Be known for your acceptance, warmth, and frequent expressions of love.

A Passionate Romance with Your Chosen Mate. And may you make the marvelous discovery that when infatuation fades, a deeper, richer passion—yes, one even beyond your wildest dreams—can take infatuation's place and make it pale against the crimson heat of love that really lasts.

Generosity in Marriage. Be a giver. When you let your spouse win, you both win. Each day, think of a way to please your mate, and do it. Other-centeredness not only makes a marriage work, but it will enlarge your individual spirit, as well.

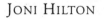

Willingness to Talk. Nearly every problem that arises in marriage can be solved if both partners are eager to communicate and find solutions. This same principle applies to the workplace, neighborhoods, friendships, and parenting.

Friends to Love. May you find and keep friends who feel like family. May they be more than mere acquaintances, more than passing trains. May they earn your highest trust, and be the sort of companions you would go into battle with and for. The truth is, you're already there. Surround yourself with friends who treat you with genuine love.

Spontaneity. Discover the joy of surprises, and be willing to embark on sudden adventures. Don't be scheduled so tightly that you step back from the carefree larks that often lead us to our happiest memories. Let excitement take you by the hand, and it will show you laughter and delight that you never knew were there.

Joie de Vivre—The Joy of Living. May you plunge into life each day with enthusiasm and cheer, having a buoyant lilt in your step and a zestful approach to all you do. May this sunny outlook radiate from you in an irresistible wave, like rings from a pebble tossed exuberantly into a pond, rippling happily over all who surround you.

Simple Pleasures. May the memory of a kind word carry you for a whole week. May you savor the sweetness of an ice cream cone, and never eat one quickly. May you swell with admiration at even rows of crops beside the road. May you grin at children and scratch behind the ears of dogs. May you rave about delicious meals and jobs well done. Always find the sublime in the simple. Cherish not only every rainbow, but every drop of rain that brought it forth.

A Sense of Humor. Look for the amusing side of life's ups and downs (especially the downs). It's always there, and will see you through many of life's storms. Take time to laugh, especially at yourself. Refuse to take yourself too seriously. Develop a wry wit that can take mundane events and make them utterly hilarious.

Delight in Uniqueness. You are of infinite value, truly a wondrous individual. You are special not only to me, but to the world. There has never been anyone exactly like you, ever in history. And there will never be another to follow who is all that you are. There is only one you. Revel in your own personality; find your voice and stay true to it.

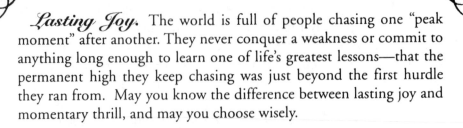

Lasting Joy. The world is full of people chasing one "peak moment" after another. They never conquer a weakness or commit to anything long enough to learn one of life's greatest lessons—that the permanent high they keep chasing was just beyond the first hurdle they ran from. May you know the difference between lasting joy and momentary thrill, and may you choose wisely.

A Forgiving Heart. May you relinquish grudges and always give people another chance. Those who are enslaved by resentment will never taste the sweet freedom—and even the personal power—that comes when we truly forgive each other.

Tolerance. Allow for—and even celebrate—the differences you find in others. Live your way with determination, but never require others to choose your same path. Remember that individuality is virtually sacred, and must be preserved by the seemingly trivial act of living—and letting others live.

Patience. You cannot savor if you rush, and savoring is vital to good living. Be willing to wait for the rose to bloom. Let those without your same gifts take the time they need, and know that the genius who is impatient with others is really no genius at all. Instead, she is one who has missed the whole garden while tearing open a bud.

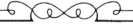

A Long Fuse. Be slow to anger, always assuming the other person has a noble motive for his actions. Make one up! You will be amazed at the peace and calm you'll feel. Do not take offense, even when offense is intended. Pity the malicious, and refuse to join them. If your anger is justified, put it into a plan of action rather than into a self-pitying outburst. Strive for an even disposition and a cool temperament. When we lose control, we lose all. It is the ultimate defeat.

A Careful Tongue. A heart pierced by sharp words is very slow to heal. Think before you speak, and banish criticism from your conversation. Refuse to find fault with yourself or others. May words that build and comfort be your gifts to those around you.

The Ability to Apologize. One hallmark of true greatness is the willingness to admit our own errors and to seek another's forgiveness. The inability to say "I'm sorry" has left a trail of broken hearts, lost jobs, and destroyed relationships. Be the first to apologize in a quarrel. It's the only way to truly win one.

A Logical Mind. May you be blessed with the ability to think clearly and with strong reasoning. May your intelligence spare you time and suffering as you make wise judgments and decisions. And may this ability make you more observant and creative, too.

The Sound of Bells. May you find yourself stopping, amid the rush and clamor of life, to gaze up and listen to a canopy of chimes. They could come from a huge bell tower, a village square, or a church steeple. But may they always delight you, slow you down, and make you smile.

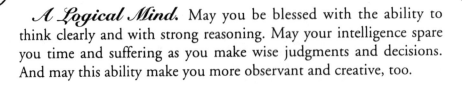
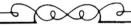

Fresh Sheets. May your day end with peaceful slumber as you settle into clean, cottony fragrance and smooth, crisp coverings. Take pride in making a beautiful bed. Buy the best pillow you can afford. You'll be spending almost half your life on it.

A Good Journal. Choose a beautiful, well-bound cover, high quality paper, and a writing pen you really love. Take the time to fill its pages with your triumphs and your sorrows, even daily details that might seem mundane. Keeping a journal is good therapy, and your posterity will cherish it forever.

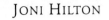

Spring Bulbs. Take the time to plant daffodils, tulips, and irises. There is nothing so life-affirming, so optimistic, and so reassuring as the serenade of spring's first blossoms, coming forth in perfect trust that winter will end, and warmth return.

A Devoted Dog. And he must have huge brown eyes that look up at you with unconditional love, even if it seems that all others have let you down. He must have a tail that wags faster for you than it does for anyone else. Shown any love at all, a dog will defend you to its death. They possess a loyalty and a devotion that makes it perfectly all right to let them sleep on the bed.

One Truly Inspiring Song. This is the tune you will hum in your head whenever you need strength, comfort, and a reminder that you are a winner. Let it cheer you up when you feel sad; let it invigorate you as you approach a breathtaking challenge. Let it center you and pull your personality into its truest, happiest form.

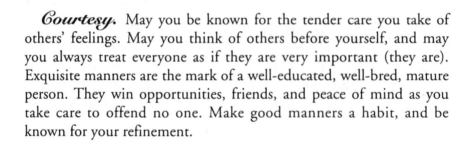

Courtesy. May you be known for the tender care you take of others' feelings. May you think of others before yourself, and may you always treat everyone as if they are very important (they are). Exquisite manners are the mark of a well-educated, well-bred, mature person. They win opportunities, friends, and peace of mind as you take care to offend no one. Make good manners a habit, and be known for your refinement.

Discernment. Be one who can see beyond the surface of a situation to the reality underneath. Know right from wrong, even when the line looks blurred to others. You will solve problems with less effort and emerge as one who is sharp, hard to fool, and worthy of many followers.

Caution. In your energy and enthusiasm, may you slow down at the big intersections—the places where important decisions are made. Weigh the sides carefully, lest you leap into the arms of error; recklessness always results in disaster. Then, once you have exercised caution, make your decision and do not waver.

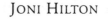

Tact. May you always be able to say the difficult things with love and respect. May your quick mind not create a quick tongue, but an array of choices that come quickly to mind, so that you may always choose the kindest.

Charm. May others find you fascinating, a delight to be around. The charm must be genuine, not manufactured for the purpose of gathering followers. Charm will grant you opportunity, friendships, romance—and it can even subdue your enemies.

Dignity. May you always respond nobly to detractors, and always display class. Do more than merely "the right thing." Do it with no thought of recognition. Erase all desire to get even, and just be your best.

Hot Breakfasts. Start your day with a good meal, unhurried if you can. Morning is a productive time, and one which requires the finest fuel. Don't shortchange yourself by grabbing a partial breakfast on the run. Learn to make good omelets, fluffy pancakes, and fresh juice.

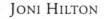

A Productive Garden. Even if all you have is a window sill or a row of pots, learn to grow vegetables. Not only will your fresh produce taste delicious, but you will gain respect for the earth, and for the miracle of seeds, and how they possess an intelligence that knows precisely when and how to become a carrot.

Elegant Desserts. Don't have one every day, but indulge on occasion in a rich, delicious finish to your meal. Don't live the deprived existence of a lifetime dieter; splurge now and then. To live an enjoyable life, one's eyes should dance occasionally.

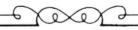

An Inviting Table. Light candles. Take time to make your eating area special. Make others feel eminently welcome there, and break bread with many people through your lifetime. You will get to know people more intimately as you share meals and conversation with them, than in almost any other way.

An Adventurous Palate. Don't be a finicky bore who only likes one or two vegetables, and who refuses to eat anything that could possibly contain sour cream. Be fun to eat with, be an interesting dining companion. Dare to try new dishes and edible discoveries; you'll find all kinds of foods you like, and enjoy a lifetime of variety in your meals.

Triumph over Adversity. I know that life's most precious lessons are often learned the hard way, through stark adversity. And yet, because I love you and would ache to see you in pain, I suppose I would wish to remove all life's difficulties from your path. Perhaps it's a good thing that such a wish can never come true. You will, of course, experience mishaps; I simply hope that you will prove greater than your trials. May you rise from the crushing blows of life a shining victor—wiser from the battle's lessons, stronger for its toll.

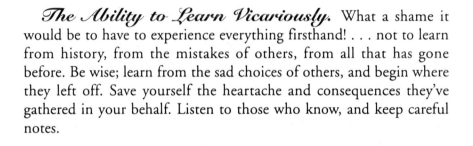

The Ability to Learn Vicariously. What a shame it would be to have to experience everything firsthand! . . . not to learn from history, from the mistakes of others, from all that has gone before. Be wise; learn from the sad choices of others, and begin where they left off. Save yourself the heartache and consequences they've gathered in your behalf. Listen to those who know, and keep careful notes.

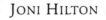

Decisiveness. After careful consideration of your options, demonstrate strength and resolve. Make a decision and don't look back. Even if you are occasionally wrong, it is better to make a decision and move ahead than to hang back, wringing your hands as others pass you by. And never be indecisive when ordering lunch. Lunch is not that important.

Hindsight. Don't constantly glance backward or dwell upon the past; one must move on. But it is a gift to learn from the past, to see where the mistake was so that you can prevent it the next time around.

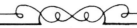

Assertiveness. May you, with supreme kindness, state your thoughts and feelings as you have them, without anguishing over times when you wish you had been more forthright. Stand up for yourself and for what you believe. Never bully or offend, simply be plain and direct.

Success. May you attain the noble goals you hold within your heart, and feel the joy of accomplishment. But may your greatest success be in your relationships with your loved ones. This success— success of the soul—is much greater than financial success.

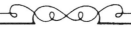

Eloquence When You Really Need It. May the words come to you in a beautiful tapestry when you are defending the right, speaking before a group, complimenting another, or having a disagreement. May you not only organize your thoughts and express yourself clearly, but may you be enchanting to your listeners and persuasive in your speech.

Expressions of Gratitude. Be generous with your thanks, never letting even the smallest act of kindness slip by unacknowledged. Show appreciation in every way you can, and walk through life with a grateful heart.

Hospitality to Visitors. Make all feel welcome within your home. Put aside your other activities and concentrate on your guests. Make their favorite foods. Give them your finest linens and put a treat on their pillow. Be a generous host, and never let your guests go hungry or thirsty. Make them feel as though they've stepped into a corner of heaven when they step into your home.

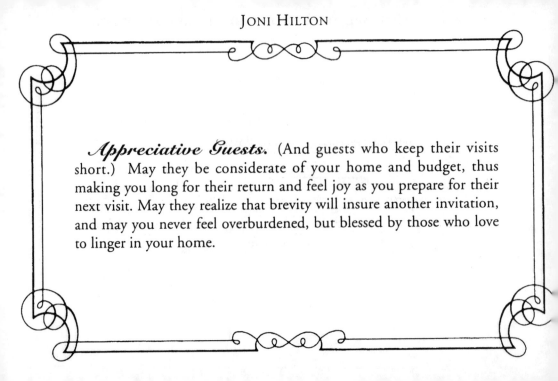

Appreciative Guests. (And guests who keep their visits short.) May they be considerate of your home and budget, thus making you long for their return and feel joy as you prepare for their next visit. May they realize that brevity will insure another invitation, and may you never feel overburdened, but blessed by those who love to linger in your home.

Someone to Write Letters To. There is something beautiful about a handwritten page, lifted from an envelope and unfolded to reveal a friend's latest news. Too many of our relationships come and go through phone calls and visits, with never a written word passing between us. It is a lost art. Recapture it, savor it, and share it. Letters form a facet of friendship for which there is truly no substitute.

Brilliant Compromises. May you be blessed with the ability to mediate for others, to see options others overlook, and to find common ground amid disagreement. May others seek your counsel and find ultimate fairness in your arbitration.

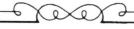

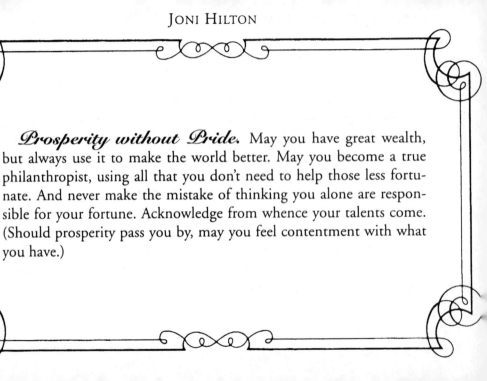

Prosperity without Pride. May you have great wealth, but always use it to make the world better. May you become a true philanthropist, using all that you don't need to help those less fortunate. And never make the mistake of thinking you alone are responsible for your fortune. Acknowledge from whence your talents come. (Should prosperity pass you by, may you feel contentment with what you have.)

Quality. Learn to recognize that which lasts, and buy the best you can afford. Shun the trendy and the cheaply made. Recognize real value, and be willing to pay its price. Better to have five well-made, timeless, and classic garments than a closet full of quickly outdated fashions. The same goes for furnishings and automobiles.

Simplicity. True elegance avoids clutter and excess ornamentation. It is not only the mark of class, it is the mark of one who is content with himself.

Style. May you have impeccable taste, unhomogenized by the dictates of experts. May your home and clothing reflect real personality—a distinctive style that is all your own.

Terrific Bargains. May your life be sprinkled with delicious moments when you happen upon astoundingly low prices. (And may you always have the discretion not to bore your friends with your excited telling of the event.)

Lilacs. They are the embodiment of delicacy in color, form, and fragrance. Take time to bury your face in their blossoms and inhale deeply. Learn that subtle is always more alluring than bold.

Honey on Hot Bread. Surround yourself with homey smells and tastes. Sip cocoa by a fire. Drizzle butter over fresh popcorn. Lick spoonfuls of cookie dough. Let all these scents and flavors intertwine with happy memories to recall and savor all your life.

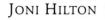

Summer Rain. May your sunkissed face turn up in delight as dark clouds gather and burst, quenching and cooling, soaking into thirsty ground and creating a vivid coat of green on every hillside all around.

Tranquil, Lavender Evenings. May you pause during that sundown moment when dusk removes all shadows, and trees stand silhouetted against pastel skies. May you feel the night begin to chill, see twinkling lights come on, and find the first star to appear. Reflect upon your day, and feel the joy of time well spent. Bid your day goodbye with a grateful heart, and turn to embrace the night. It will renew you for the morrow.

Apple Blossoms. With any luck, you'll find an orchard full. There is something mesmerizing about the lacy shawl these trees weave overhead. Until they work their blossomy magic, they look gnarled and ugly, incapable of bringing forth beauty. Yet, there it is. Learn the lesson of the apple trees, and judge no one by appearance. Know, too, that after beauty come the richest fruits of all.

Thunder and Lightning. What is more invigorating than a mighty storm, crashing and illuminating the sky, penetrating your very soul? Human beings will always be at nature's mercy, awed by her power, prayerful to have her on our side, and fortunate to observe such a magnificent performance.

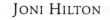

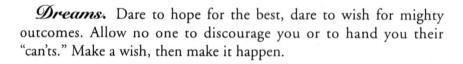

Dreams. Dare to hope for the best, dare to wish for mighty outcomes. Allow no one to discourage you or to hand you their "can'ts." Make a wish, then make it happen.

Vision. Be guided by your determination to make your dreams come true. Picture the world in a better state. Visualize yourself achieving your goals. Don't hold back from imagining the glorious possibilities you can turn into realities. Every great achievement began as a single thought.

Heroes. May you feel genuine admiration for people you know—people who will influence you throughout your life. May you emulate the best of them, and ask yourself, "What would my hero do in this situation?"

Purpose. While others drift, you can be the one who drives. Pull out of the coasting zone and into the passing lane. Know what you want, and be able to outline your path to get it. Have concrete goals, not vague ones. Have short goals that inch you toward your larger goals. And remember that direction is vastly more important than speed.

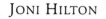

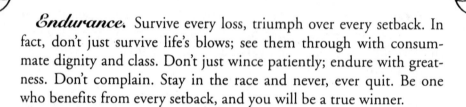

Endurance. Survive every loss, triumph over every setback. In fact, don't just survive life's blows; see them through with consummate dignity and class. Don't just wince patiently; endure with greatness. Don't complain. Stay in the race and never, ever quit. Be one who benefits from every setback, and you will be a true winner.

Fulfillment. May you feel satisfaction as you attain your goals and find your efforts well rewarded. May all the parts of your life bring you joy and contentment, and may frustration only last long enough to ensure action.

A Noble Heritage. Everyone has one, you know. If they can't find it by looking at their immediate ancestors, they simply need to look further back on the family tree. Eventually you'll find someone to admire, someone who makes you thrill as you think that you share their genes, blood, and inherited traits. Appreciate your relatives and the sacrifices they made for the freedoms you enjoy. Delight in your identity, nationality, and customs. You come from good stock—terrific stock!

The Affection of Your Children. May you form an unbreakable bond of love and an eternal friendship with your offspring. Take time to enjoy them, to share hobbies together, to listen to them. May they show you their affection often, and may they someday give you the greatest compliment known to man: May your children admire you and like you once they're grown.

Cascading Laughter. May the humor of life tumble over you, especially when it's needed in a crisis. Never take yourself, or life's thorns, too seriously. Spend entire afternoons enraptured with giggles. Don't be afraid to laugh out loud—enjoy life! And someday, when you're old, may all your lines be smile lines.

Anonymity in Doing Good. Not even your favorite treat is as delicious as a good deed done in secret. Make it a point to conjure up wonderful acts of clandestine service. There's a certain joy in the eyes of people who do this. Their self-esteem is high, and their enjoyment of daily living surpasses everyone else's.

Optimism. Expect the best to happen, assume the best of others, and envision the best about yourself. Approach life with a cheery outlook, focusing upon the good around you. Always remember that happiness is not the result of circumstances; happiness is a choice you make.

Deep Feelings. May you dedicate yourself to noble causes and solid convictions. May your heart pound, your pulse race, and your eyes water with joy, love, respect, and even righteous anger. Never suppress sensitivity. To live without ever experiencing a moment of intense emotion is not to live at all.

The Ability to Lift Others' Spirits. May you have the rare gift of contagious joy. May others be drawn to you because of the lilting encouragement and inspiring gladness you radiate. May you have the knack of being able to say exactly the right thing to turn someone from despair to hope. Be a motivator. There is nothing so magnetic as one who makes us feel great about ourselves.

An Infectious Smile. It's such a simple, easy gift. Giving a great smile away creates a ripple effect. You'll never know how many smiles resulted from the one you gave to a shopkeeper, a boy on the bus, an executive in an elevator. What's more, your own mood follows the expression on your face. Make yours a cheerful countenance.

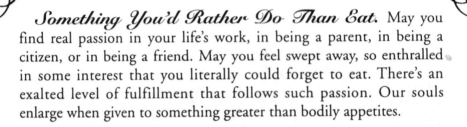

Something You'd Rather Do Than Eat. May you find real passion in your life's work, in being a parent, in being a citizen, or in being a friend. May you feel swept away, so enthralled in some interest that you literally could forget to eat. There's an exalted level of fulfillment that follows such passion. Our souls enlarge when given to something greater than bodily appetites.

Spirit. Approach life with genuine zeal, with vigor and energy. Walk a little faster than average. Read a little more. Try a little harder. Be enthusiastic, even about your thoughts. Give everything you do your very best effort.

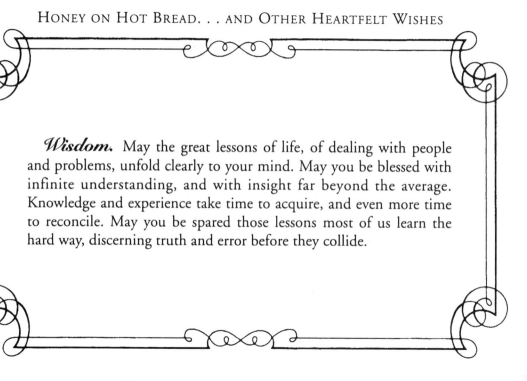

Wisdom. May the great lessons of life, of dealing with people and problems, unfold clearly to your mind. May you be blessed with infinite understanding, and with insight far beyond the average. Knowledge and experience take time to acquire, and even more time to reconcile. May you be spared those lessons most of us learn the hard way, discerning truth and error before they collide.

Inspiration. May you fine-tune your ability to hear the still, small voice that will guide you if you listen. Never be too hurried—or too sure of your own wisdom—that you turn your back on outside messages. They can elevate you, instruct you, warn you, and comfort you. Spiritual communication is your road map to all good things as you sojourn through life.

Trust in Your Hunches. One of the hardest things to learn in life is to follow your hunches. They're almost always right. Believe in your own instincts, your own intuitive reactions. Don't discard first impressions too quickly. When something doesn't feel right, pay attention. Don't lose the wonderful ability children have to size up a situation immediately and correctly.

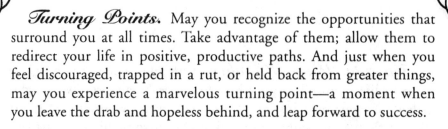

Turning Points. May you recognize the opportunities that surround you at all times. Take advantage of them; allow them to redirect your life in positive, productive paths. And just when you feel discouraged, trapped in a rut, or held back from greater things, may you experience a marvelous turning point—a moment when you leave the drab and hopeless behind, and leap forward to success.

Quiet Strolls. Some of your greatest thoughts and observations will come when you are simply taking time to enjoy life one step at a time. Learn the sounds of a country road, the beat of a city street, the dappled shade of a woodland path. Listen for swallows, smell the jasmine, feel the passing breezes.

Soothing Sounds. May you find sweet respite from the blaring noises that fill our world—traffic, telephones, radios, construction, and all the rest. May you relish the rhythmic cadences of a lawnmower on a summer day, children laughing on a playground, and ocean waves rolling on the sand. May serenity wrap its quiet arms around you and whisper gently in your ear.

Silver Mornings. May you awaken early enough to see glistening dew upon the grass, and find birds still sleeping, heads tucked under their wings. May you see a valley nestled in mist, violet against green hills. And then, may the first fingers of the sunrise stretch across a pale pink sky, beckon flowers to open, and turn your world to gold.

Solitude. May you make time, amid your many activities, to be alone with yourself. Be infinitely comfortable without a crowd, alone but not lonely. Be a cherished friend to yourself, someone you love to be with. Use this time to reflect, to evaluate your character and growth. Set new goals, develop your talents, forgive yourself.

Appreciation of Animals. Marvel at the amazing creatures who share this world with you, and respect each one in its daily struggle for survival. Decide to protect them, as they cannot do it for themselves. Be considerate of all who live, and learn from even the smallest ant.

Leisure. Of course you want to be industrious, ambitious, and determined. But without rejuvenating breaks, you become little more than a programmed robot. Take the time to relax, to slow down and play. Rediscover your childhood and throw off adult inhibitions. Splash in a puddle, play marbles, order a triple scoop. Those who do will take renewed energy back to work, and their families will take happy memories home with them.

Patriotism. Love your country and all who fought—and continue to fight—to secure its Constitution. Study its history and gain a real appreciation for your citizenship. May you thrill to see our flag as it waves against the sky, and may every singing of the national anthem bring tears to your eyes.

Political Caring. Study the issues and form your opinions after careful analysis, regardless of what others think. Stay away from the cynical. Know that one person really can make a difference, and never miss the chance to vote. Write your legislators and contribute to those you believe in.

Community Involvement. Feel a part of your neighborhood. Pick up garbage, wave to other residents, support local festivals and ball games. Visit City Hall and campaign for local improvements. Find a cause bigger than yourself and show others that by working together, you can make your neighborhood safer, happier, and more beautiful.

Action to Right Wrongs. When you see injustice, never look the other way. Have courage to fight for what is right and defend the underdog. While others talk, you be the one to do. Simply knowing right from wrong is not enough; you must couple that knowledge with fearless action.

Absence of Prejudice. Fill your life with people of all colors and religions. Get to know them and see that all have innate intelligence, all have innate goodness, all have innate value and deserve your respect. Never judge a person by appearances, and speak up to correct others who do.

Value as a Neighbor. It is a great badge of honor to be thought of as a good neighbor. Kindness on occasion is easy; but to be known as consistently thoughtful, by those who live beside you day to day, is a true measure of one's character. Look for opportunities to serve your neighbors. Never be too busy to see a need and meet it. Wave and smile when you pass, take over a plate of brownies now and then. Offer to watch their house while they're away, and be the kind of neighbor you have always wanted to have.

A Bright Countenance. May the books you read, the values you live, and the people you admire all be evident from the glow of purity in your face. May your eyes sparkle with health and your smile shine with sincerity. There is a brilliance, a glimmer of something divine, in the faces of those who surround themselves with the best they can find, and who then become the best they can be.

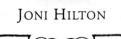

Radiant Beauty. If you possess inner peace and love for your fellowman, it will shine forth from your face, and your appearance will be dazzling. Even if your features are plain, you will look beautiful because of the joy you radiate. And, should you be fair of feature, you will seem just that much more attractive. You will always be pleased with the reflection you see in the mirror if you stay true to the noblest thoughts, feelings, and behavior you know.

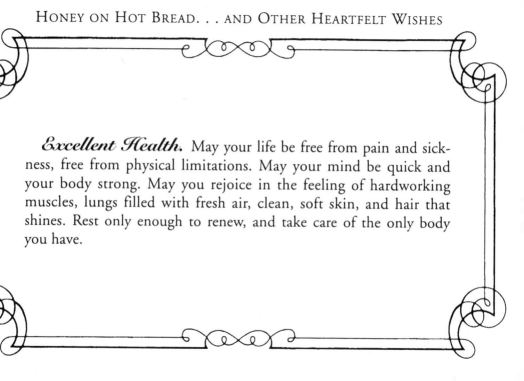

Excellent Health. May your life be free from pain and sickness, free from physical limitations. May your mind be quick and your body strong. May you rejoice in the feeling of hardworking muscles, lungs filled with fresh air, clean, soft skin, and hair that shines. Rest only enough to renew, and take care of the only body you have.

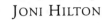

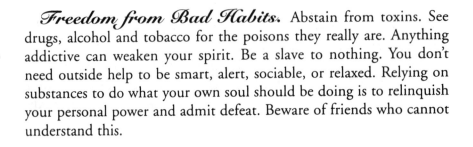

Freedom from Bad Habits. Abstain from toxins. See drugs, alcohol and tobacco for the poisons they really are. Anything addictive can weaken your spirit. Be a slave to nothing. You don't need outside help to be smart, alert, sociable, or relaxed. Relying on substances to do what your own soul should be doing is to relinquish your personal power and admit defeat. Beware of friends who cannot understand this.

Moderation. Avoid extremes. Don't join every crusade, try every diet, or follow every fad that comes along. Set your own pace and stay away from fringe fanaticism. Don't exercise until you drop, don't fast until your knees buckle, don't eat yourself sick, and don't spend until you're broke. Hold back. Slow down. Think. Look at the unhappy compulsive people you know, and resolve to maintain a steadier course.

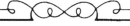

Vacations for Renewal. Even if you think you can't afford it, take your family on a yearly trip. The memories will be worth the sacrifice. Even a weekend break from your routine now and then is the perfect prevention of burn-out. Do something completely different from what you usually do. Some of your greatest laughs and funnest memories will be the travel disasters. See them as that, even while they are happening.

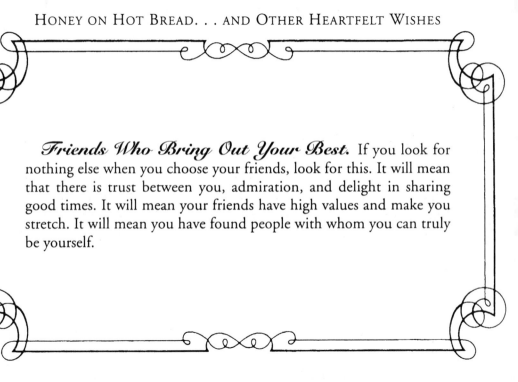

Friends Who Bring Out Your Best. If you look for nothing else when you choose your friends, look for this. It will mean that there is trust between you, admiration, and delight in sharing good times. It will mean your friends have high values and make you stretch. It will mean you have found people with whom you can truly be yourself.

Resistance to Peer Pressure. May you be so eminently satisfied with who you are that you need the approval of no one else. May you never ask yourself why you're doing something, and make the shameful discovery that it's because of what someone else will think or say. May you never lower your sights just to fit into a crowd. Crowds are groups of faceless nobodies who have sold their identity to the group.

Friendliness. Be warm, agreeable, and easy to talk to. Make others feel comfortable, welcomed, and accepted. Have a smile for everyone, and a happy wish in your heart for their success. Don't have to be right all the time, or to set the record straight. Forget yourself and get lost in your fascination with others. Everyone can teach you something; everyone has a great story.

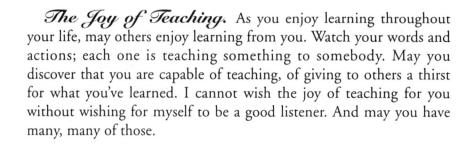

The Joy of Teaching. As you enjoy learning throughout your life, may others enjoy learning from you. Watch your words and actions; each one is teaching something to somebody. May you discover that you are capable of teaching, of giving to others a thirst for what you've learned. I cannot wish the joy of teaching for you without wishing for myself to be a good listener. And may you have many, many of those.

Acceptance. Although I hope you will not crave it, I hope it will nonetheless follow you and warm your heart. We all need to feel accepted to a degree, and may the sting of rejection never find a place in your precious heart. I promise you my acceptance, my absolute admiration. May others find you equally enchanting.

Power. Too much corrupts, it is true; but may you always have just the right amount. May you know that you do indeed have a measure of control over your life—the power to correct mistakes, the power to choose happiness, the power to reach your goals. You can influence others, and may you always use your power with great compassion.

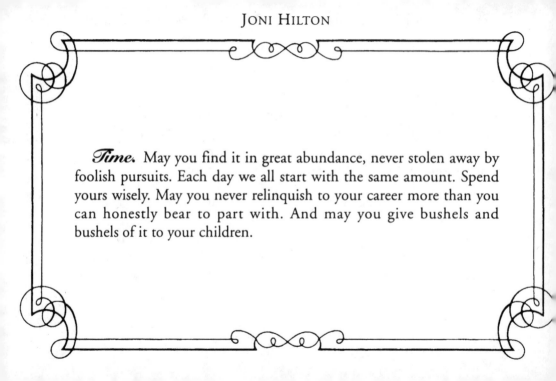

Time. May you find it in great abundance, never stolen away by foolish pursuits. Each day we all start with the same amount. Spend yours wisely. May you never relinquish to your career more than you can honestly bear to part with. And may you give bushels and bushels of it to your children.

Resistance to Judging. Give others the benefit of the doubt, and resist faultfinding. Don't let gossips dictate what you think of someone. And don't criticize people behind their backs; others will suspect that you do the same to them. Ignore others' faults, and pray they'll do the same for you. If you truly must judge another, let kindness be your measuring stick.

Foresight. Be an anticipator. Look around, size up a situation, see the pressing need and meet it. Don't have to be told the next step—not by a boss, a teacher, or a friend. Be one step ahead, and you'll soon be several miles ahead of the competition.

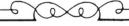

Resourcefulness. Solve problems creatively. Recycle, improvise, and invent. Anytime you hit a stumbling block or something broken, think of three solutions to the problem, three ways to fix it. Then pick the best one.

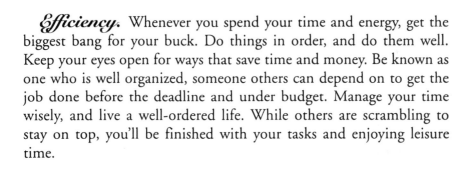

Efficiency. Whenever you spend your time and energy, get the biggest bang for your buck. Do things in order, and do them well. Keep your eyes open for ways that save time and money. Be known as one who is well organized, someone others can depend on to get the job done before the deadline and under budget. Manage your time wisely, and live a well-ordered life. While others are scrambling to stay on top, you'll be finished with your tasks and enjoying leisure time.

Thoroughness. Always finish what you start, and make every effort your polished best. Pay attention to details. Be the one who remembers to write a thank-you note, the one who notices that someone went to extra trouble, the one who insists on the highest quality, especially from yourself.

Responsibility. May you rise to every one you're given. Show that you can be trusted, that you use good judgment and maturity. Do what you say you will. And when you're in the wrong, show your strength and wisdom by speaking up quickly to take full blame. Accepting proper responsibility ends the argument and begins the process of learning.

Charity. Charity is not just an act; it's an attitude. Compassion for humanity is more than a yearly donation to a worthy cause, or a dollar tossed casually to a beggar. It's an entire way of living, of looking at your fellowman. It directs your daily actions and the heartbeats behind them. Charity makes you not only willing to sacrifice for others, but grateful for the opportunity. Strive always for greater love, greater forgiveness, greater benevolence to all.

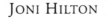

Generosity to the Poor. Give to the outstretched hand. Aren't we all beggars of a sort? If you worry that money will be misused, give coupons for fast food or buy the person a meal. It is impossible to know another's heart, and we cannot rightly judge those in need. Even if you feel sure a beggar is a fraud, give. A liar will always be in a much more pitiful position than you are. Remember: Your test is whether you will give. The beggar's honesty is his test. You only need to worry about your own.

Physical Labor. The soul is magnified through honest sweat; it is the antidote to laziness. A willingness to work and struggle will serve you over and over again in your life. It can even save marriages through determination to work just a little harder. And it is often the key to a good opinion of yourself; through your hard efforts, you will accomplish much to be proud of.

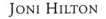

The Joy of Sacrifice. Unless you feel joy, you haven't given enough. Real sacrifice always returns more than is given. It's one of the few pieces of genuine magic floating about our universe, for it disguises itself as a hardship, and turns out to be a monumental blessing. Those who do not understand this principle have not yet tasted true sacrifice. It must be a choice you make, not an affliction thrust upon you. And it must be costly and inconvenient. It can even make you question your sanity for a moment. But, if seen through, it yields a joyous miracle. (Parenting is a good example.)

Independence. There's a tingling delight in this—a sureness of self, a great feeling of being whole. To need no one is delicious. All your relationships can then be chosen relationships, instead of pairings of entrapment. Freedom from dependence upon others (for money, for housing, for safety, for affection) is a freedom that almost defines real living. Gain knowledge, skills, and virtues that can ensure your independence. Trust yourself, by yourself.

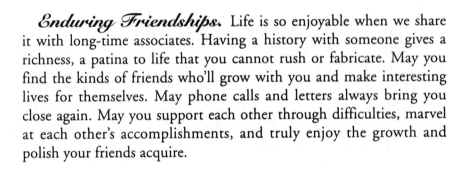

Enduring Friendships. Life is so enjoyable when we share it with long-time associates. Having a history with someone gives a richness, a patina to life that you cannot rush or fabricate. May you find the kinds of friends who'll grow with you and make interesting lives for themselves. May phone calls and letters always bring you close again. May you support each other through difficulties, marvel at each other's accomplishments, and truly enjoy the growth and polish your friends acquire.

Multiple Careers. May you discover not just one, but myriad talents to explore and refine. May your life be filled with a variety of opportunities and endless ways to earn your way in this world. Seek exposure to many fields, and prepare for a long life with many exciting twists and turns.

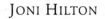

The Ability to Remember People's Names. Nothing is so musical as the sound of one's own name. Use people's names often when you meet them, and devise ways to remember who they are. Drop your concern over self, and focus upon others. Make notes later, if that will help. This skill is one anybody can develop, and it can often mean the difference between getting ahead or falling behind.

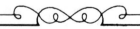

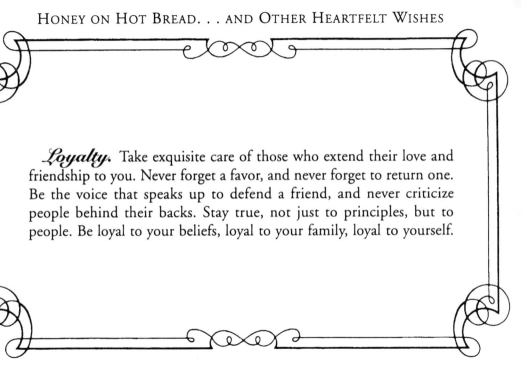

Loyalty. Take exquisite care of those who extend their love and friendship to you. Never forget a favor, and never forget to return one. Be the voice that speaks up to defend a friend, and never criticize people behind their backs. Stay true, not just to principles, but to people. Be loyal to your beliefs, loyal to your family, loyal to yourself.

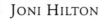

Maturity. If you develop this one before you're old, you'll save yourself a lot of grief. Be able to defer gratification, and let others go first. Be slow to anger and have no need to prove anything, especially while driving. Develop a sophisticated sense of humor that never delights in belittling others. See setbacks in their proper context, not as earth-shattering events. Avoid panic, silly outbursts, and excessive concern over yourself. (Not only are other people not judging you every minute; they aren't even thinking about you.)

Wariness of Free Lunches. Be a shrewd observer of life's fluttering parade of sales pitches. Don't be led into a trap by grand promises. Remember, if something sounds too good to be true, it probably is. Avoid greed; it leads us to grab a juicy plum without first checking for a bumblebee. When something is offered with "no strings attached," ask yourself why they had to mention that.

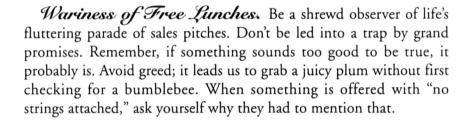

Conflict with Evil. Never be comfortable with that which is wrong. Don't laugh at those who talk about driving drunk, don't shrug when a friend brags about his phony insurance claim. Be principled. See the line clearly between right and wrong. Even if growing numbers think the line has blurred, it hasn't. Stay firmly planted in the center of moral ethics, distancing yourself from the cliff's edge. Avoid overexposure to compromising lifestyles; it can lead to a numbing indifference, and finally, acceptance.

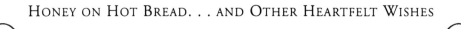

Good Advice. As you search for solutions throughout your life, may you be surrounded by wise friends and advisors who will guide you well. Watch out for "expert opinions"; you'll often get a different opinion from each expert you ask. May you discern between good advice and bad, and may you always remember that the final choice is still yours.

Beautiful Surroundings. Take pride in your home and workplace. Be more than just neat and clean; take time to arrange fresh flowers in a vase. Display your favorite art. Let lovely music and inviting aromas fill the air. Your home doesn't have to look like a photograph from a magazine, but it should feel inviting and eye-pleasing to you. Our surroundings affect our moods; choose colors and belongings that make you smile.

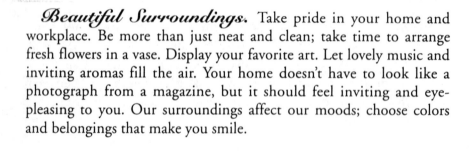

Good Neighbors. May your neighbors be considerate, keep orderly yards, and share extra cookies with you, fresh from the oven! May they never have loud parties late into the night, or dogs that bark when a breeze goes by. May you become friends with your neighbors, correspond when one of you moves, and watch with delight as their children grow.

A Favorite Sport. May you be strong and athletic, truly able to enjoy the sports you try. May you become proficient at many, and superb in at least one. May you learn from the dedication and practice this requires, and may it fill a corner of your life as no other activity can.

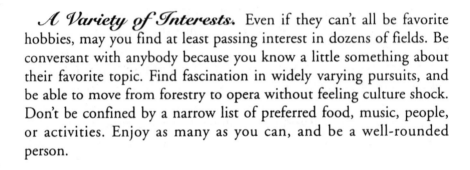

A Variety of Interests. Even if they can't all be favorite hobbies, may you find at least passing interest in dozens of fields. Be conversant with anybody because you know a little something about their favorite topic. Find fascination in widely varying pursuits, and be able to move from forestry to opera without feeling culture shock. Don't be confined by a narrow list of preferred food, music, people, or activities. Enjoy as many as you can, and be a well-rounded person.

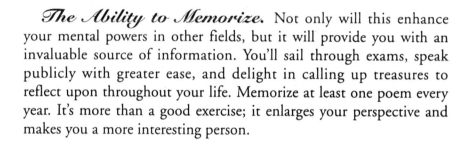

The Ability to Memorize. Not only will this enhance your mental powers in other fields, but it will provide you with an invaluable source of information. You'll sail through exams, speak publicly with greater ease, and delight in calling up treasures to reflect upon throughout your life. Memorize at least one poem every year. It's more than a good exercise; it enlarges your perspective and makes you a more interesting person.

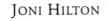

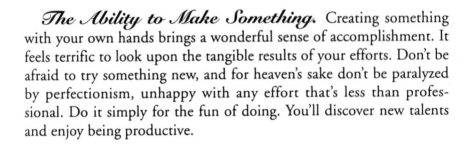

The Ability to Make Something. Creating something with your own hands brings a wonderful sense of accomplishment. It feels terrific to look upon the tangible results of your efforts. Don't be afraid to try something new, and for heaven's sake don't be paralyzed by perfectionism, unhappy with any effort that's less than professional. Do it simply for the fun of doing. You'll discover new talents and enjoy being productive.

New Experiences. May you greet change with an open mind and eagerness of spirit. Don't recoil simply because something is new or different; see it as an adventure. Life surprises us with job transfers, new opportunities, and sudden bends in the road. Be adaptable! Forge ahead; expect to find good, and to learn from each new experience you have.

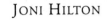

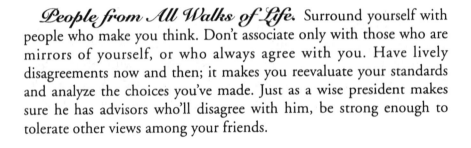

People from All Walks of Life. Surround yourself with people who make you think. Don't associate only with those who are mirrors of yourself, or who always agree with you. Have lively disagreements now and then; it makes you reevaluate your standards and analyze the choices you've made. Just as a wise president makes sure he has advisors who'll disagree with him, be strong enough to tolerate other views among your friends.

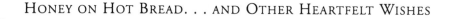

Kindness. Make your first thought in dealing with others, "What is the kindest thing to do here?" Don't worry about being offended; take great care not to offend. Everyone has sensitive feelings, and the most loving act of all is to consider the delicate soul within another. Seek opportunities to extend a hand, to give someone another chance. Never miss the opportunity to do a good deed, however small. You may never have this chance again.

Tenderness. May you be strong, yes, but may you never forget to be tender—for this is the greatest strength. Learn the power in a gentle touch, the wiping of a tear, the kissing of a hurt, the stroking of a weary head. Hold the wavering hand, whisper the encouraging word, take the extra moment to embrace. Others will forget your take-charge moments of assertive command, but they will always remember the time you took them aside, put your arm around them, and comforted them when they hurt.

Understanding of Others. We cannot read others' minds, or see an event through their eyes. But may you be blessed with the gift of empathy, of being able to glimpse a greater portion of others' hearts, and truly come to understand them. When we fully understand others, we cannot resist loving them. In the perfect light of understanding, they become whole—people with attributes and flaws alike (just like us) who are nevertheless forgivable and loveable. And may you also know others equally blessed, who genuinely understand you.

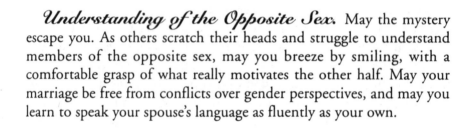

Understanding of the Opposite Sex. May the mystery escape you. As others scratch their heads and struggle to understand members of the opposite sex, may you breeze by smiling, with a comfortable grasp of what really motivates the other half. May your marriage be free from conflicts over gender perspectives, and may you learn to speak your spouse's language as fluently as your own.

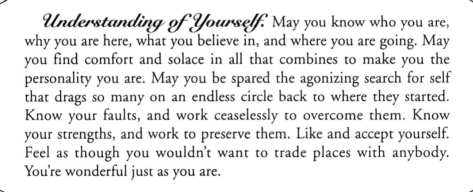

Understanding of Yourself. May you know who you are, why you are here, what you believe in, and where you are going. May you find comfort and solace in all that combines to make you the personality you are. May you be spared the agonizing search for self that drags so many on an endless circle back to where they started. Know your faults, and work ceaselessly to overcome them. Know your strengths, and work to preserve them. Like and accept yourself. Feel as though you wouldn't want to trade places with anybody. You're wonderful just as you are.

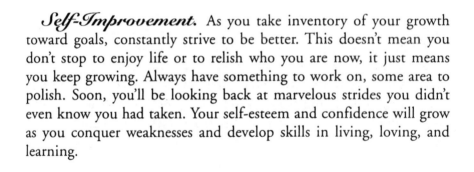

Self-Improvement. As you take inventory of your growth toward goals, constantly strive to be better. This doesn't mean you don't stop to enjoy life or to relish who you are now, it just means you keep growing. Always have something to work on, some area to polish. Soon, you'll be looking back at marvelous strides you didn't even know you had taken. Your self-esteem and confidence will grow as you conquer weaknesses and develop skills in living, loving, and learning.

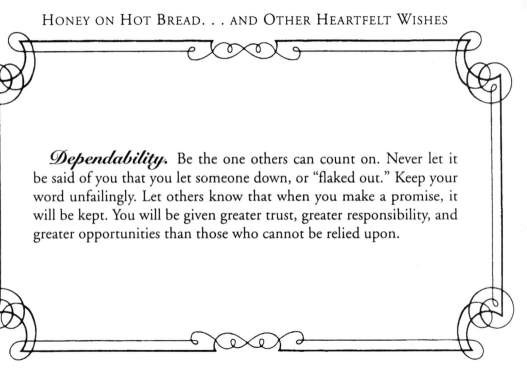

Dependability. Be the one others can count on. Never let it be said of you that you let someone down, or "flaked out." Keep your word unfailingly. Let others know that when you make a promise, it will be kept. You will be given greater trust, greater responsibility, and greater opportunities than those who cannot be relied upon.

Willingness to Take Risks. Be cautious about following sudden impulses, but definitely take calculated chances. Go for the biggest, the best. Believe that you deserve success. All great leaders are great risk-takers. Occasionally, you do lose; but more often, you win. If you never try, you simply cannot win. Those who hang back in the "safe zone" eventually find themselves moaning about "the one that got away." Go after what you want, and give it your best shot.

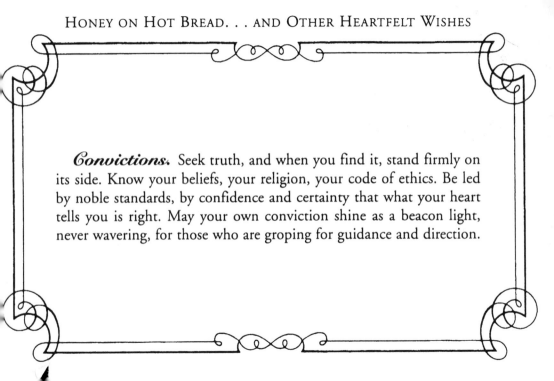

Convictions. Seek truth, and when you find it, stand firmly on its side. Know your beliefs, your religion, your code of ethics. Be led by noble standards, by confidence and certainty that what your heart tells you is right. May your own conviction shine as a beacon light, never wavering, for those who are groping for guidance and direction.

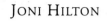

The Ability to Motivate. May you have a remarkable and most rewarding gift: the ability to improve each life you touch. Through your encouragement and enthusiasm, may others believe in themselves and resolve to reach their dreams. May you see grand potential in all those you meet, and be able to convince them of the wonderful abilities they have. People will thank you again and again for turning their lives around, for giving them wonderful ideas, and for simply taking their hand and believing in them.

Courage. This is better than bravery. Bravery is simply the willingness to be daring—to do the reckless, dangerous thing. Courage is the strength to say no. Courage is what you need to risk unpopularity, or to stand up for what's right against a crowd. It's courage that helps us make personal sacrifices for a greater good. Courage is what helps us meet sorrows in life, then helps us to pick ourselves up and go on.

Sincerity. Never indulge in false praise or self-serving flattery. Make sure the words you say are felt in your heart, and look the other person straight in the eye when you say them. When you inquire how friends are doing, take time to actively listen and ask further. (But if pressed to compliment someone's hat or cooking, always let kindness win out over sincerity.)

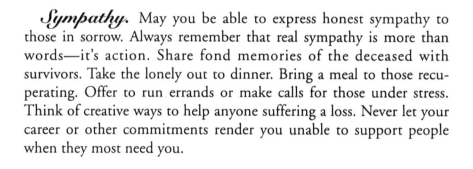

Sympathy. May you be able to express honest sympathy to those in sorrow. Always remember that real sympathy is more than words—it's action. Share fond memories of the deceased with survivors. Take the lonely out to dinner. Bring a meal to those recuperating. Offer to run errands or make calls for those under stress. Think of creative ways to help anyone suffering a loss. Never let your career or other commitments render you unable to support people when they most need you.

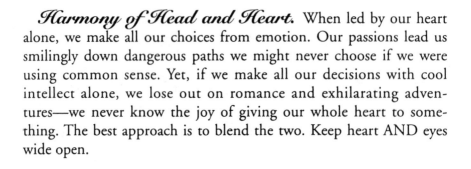

Harmony of Head and Heart. When led by our heart alone, we make all our choices from emotion. Our passions lead us smilingly down dangerous paths we might never choose if we were using common sense. Yet, if we make all our decisions with cool intellect alone, we lose out on romance and exhilarating adventures—we never know the joy of giving our whole heart to something. The best approach is to blend the two. Keep heart AND eyes wide open.

Depth. To enjoy life to its fullest, you must have layers and layers below the surface. Be able to see many facets of an event, to know in an instant that there could be half a dozen explanations or sides to the story. See things in their context, not as isolated blips in time. Don't jump to conclusions; be thoughtful. Listen to the experiences of others, and spend time reading good books. Think deeply, striving to understand and be enlightened.

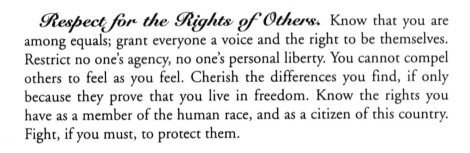

Respect for the Rights of Others. Know that you are among equals; grant everyone a voice and the right to be themselves. Restrict no one's agency, no one's personal liberty. You cannot compel others to feel as you feel. Cherish the differences you find, if only because they prove that you live in freedom. Know the rights you have as a member of the human race, and as a citizen of this country. Fight, if you must, to protect them.

Justice. Should your fate ever rest in the hands of another, may you prevail in perfect justice, never feeling slighted or victimized. And may you always deal fairly with others, never abusing power or privilege. Should you make a mistake, may you always err on the side of mercy.

Trust. May you assume the best of others, avoiding paranoia and defensiveness. Even when trust is betrayed, may you show resilience and the sense to trust again, rather than making sweeping assumptions about large groups. Don't go through life with your guard up and one foot pointed toward litigation. Avoid those who are eager to sue; you could be their next target.

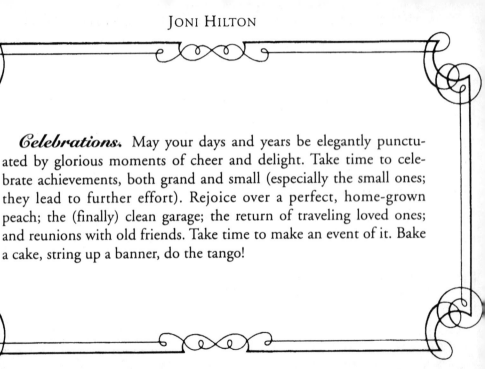

Celebrations. May your days and years be elegantly punctuated by glorious moments of cheer and delight. Take time to celebrate achievements, both grand and small (especially the small ones; they lead to further effort). Rejoice over a perfect, home-grown peach; the (finally) clean garage; the return of traveling loved ones; and reunions with old friends. Take time to make an event of it. Bake a cake, string up a banner, do the tango!

Bright Holidays. Reach your arms wide to embrace them all! Decorate to the hilt, splurge on a special gift, fill the air with music, and whip up something delicious in the kitchen. Share the occasion with those who are alone; do some service every time. Anticipate holidays with the glee of a child, and when a month is without one, make one up!

Brisk Walks. Some exercises are strictly for the body; this one includes the soul. Feel the invigoration of a confident stride, a pumping heart. Appreciate your legs and feet; breathe gratefully of crisp air and fragrant vines. Let all the parts of your body work harmoniously together in a symphony of health and vigor.

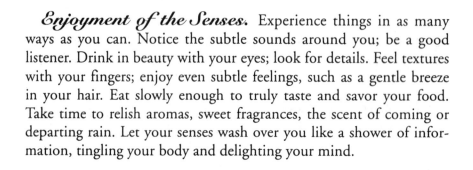

Enjoyment of the Senses. Experience things in as many ways as you can. Notice the subtle sounds around you; be a good listener. Drink in beauty with your eyes; look for details. Feel textures with your fingers; enjoy even subtle feelings, such as a gentle breeze in your hair. Eat slowly enough to truly taste and savor your food. Take time to relish aromas, sweet fragrances, the scent of coming or departing rain. Let your senses wash over you like a shower of information, tingling your body and delighting your mind.

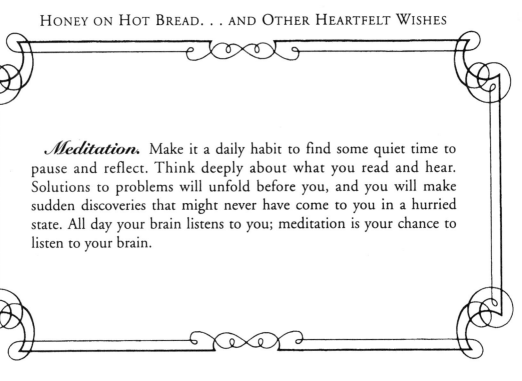

Meditation. Make it a daily habit to find some quiet time to pause and reflect. Think deeply about what you read and hear. Solutions to problems will unfold before you, and you will make sudden discoveries that might never have come to you in a hurried state. All day your brain listens to you; meditation is your chance to listen to your brain.

Unfailing Honesty. Be truthful, even to your enemies, and even when it's difficult. Remember, a lie is any effort to deceive. Don't cheat, ever. It is nearly impossible to restore trust once you have been dishonest. Let others know that you keep your word, that your handshake is your promise. Honesty is not the best policy; it's the only policy.

Noble Motives. Be free from the subtleties of a devious mind; be above board in all your dealings. Never have a secret agenda or a suspicious plan. Ask yourself, "Why am I doing this?" often, and be honest when you answer. Let your motives be for the good of mankind, for the benefit of your family, for personal improvement. Be wary of such motives as fear, obligation, fame, ease, status, wealth, revenge, or ego gratification. The greatest motive has always been love.

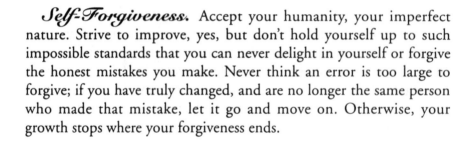

Self-Forgiveness. Accept your humanity, your imperfect nature. Strive to improve, yes, but don't hold yourself up to such impossible standards that you can never delight in yourself or forgive the honest mistakes you make. Never think an error is too large to forgive; if you have truly changed, and are no longer the same person who made that mistake, let it go and move on. Otherwise, your growth stops where your forgiveness ends.

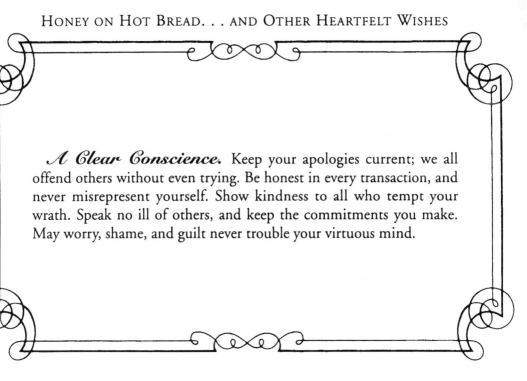

A Clear Conscience. Keep your apologies current; we all offend others without even trying. Be honest in every transaction, and never misrepresent yourself. Show kindness to all who tempt your wrath. Speak no ill of others, and keep the commitments you make. May worry, shame, and guilt never trouble your virtuous mind.

Usefulness to Others. Here's the world's best travel secret: Be constantly looking for people to help. Hold a crying baby for a mother in an airplane; let her have one moment's peace. Offer to photograph a family so they'll have at least one shot of everyone together. Recommend great restaurants and hotels. Hold the door for those struggling with luggage. No matter how many disruptions your vacation has, you'll enjoy the trip because you were other-centered. Now, take this travel tip into your journey through life. It, too, will be sprinkled with disasters, but you'll sail serenely through it because you've found the joy of service.

Light. May you live in a world where sunlight splashes all about you, lifting your spirits and carrying you high upon its wings. Invite it into your home, and pay careful attention to the way it creates moods in various rooms. Find the colors within each streak of light, the places where it reflects, and the places where it rests. Gather it about you, direct its path, and wrap yourself in its golden shawl.

Energy. May you spring into the morning when you rise, filled with vitality and brimming with great ideas. May your enthusiasm be contagious, energizing others in your wake. And may you never feel the frustration of a willing mind but a weary body. May you always have enough energy to accomplish what you wish.

Color. May your world burst with vivid hues as well as restful shades. May you respond to the colors that swirl about your world, and seek those that inspire you. Be daring—paint a room orange if you wish. Wear a purple suit. Break out of the drab, the safe. Find the colors that make your heart sing, and surround yourself with them.

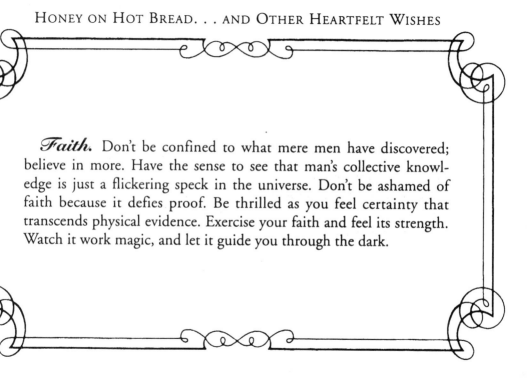

Faith. Don't be confined to what mere men have discovered; believe in more. Have the sense to see that man's collective knowledge is just a flickering speck in the universe. Don't be ashamed of faith because it defies proof. Be thrilled as you feel certainty that transcends physical evidence. Exercise your faith and feel its strength. Watch it work magic, and let it guide you through the dark.

Miracles. They're all around, but rarely noticed. Be one who sees them. Watch carefully, and you will see miracles follow faith. Don't discount the miracles so many take for granted. Appreciate the narrow escape, the healing power of love, the life of our planet, the birth of a child. May you witness many miracles in your life, and may you always recognize them for what they really are.

Reverence. Respect and honor that which is a gift to us all: our very lives. See the sacred in the common, see the spiritual in all you do. Stand in awe before a mountain, bow your head beneath the sky. Divinity leaves fingerprints upon us all.

Preparedness. Live as an optimist, but not with your head in the sand. Have the food, clothing, and fuel you would need in an emergency. Write a will and keep your financial affairs in order. Know first aid. Have another career to fall back on. Have foresight, and simply be ready for life's turnabouts, not caught off guard when storms arise.

Neatness. How you live is a reflection of your character and mind. Take pride in clean surroundings, polished shoes, organized closets, and washed cars. Your level of neatness has a great impact upon those who live with you; never burden others with a selfish lifestyle. Consider how they may want their world to look. Also, it is widely known that those who keep their personal belongings in good repair treat their relationships the same way.

Punctuality. Make it a habit to be on time; it shows respect for others' schedules. Habitual latecomers send a message of arrogant self-importance. Never treat people as inferiors. Always leave for appointments enough ahead of time so that you'll be early; this leaves a margin for emergencies and lets you arrive calmly, unlike the latecomers who always seem scattered. Be punctual in paying bills, too. Withholding money owed is the same as stealing. Be honest and pay as you go.

Sportsmanship. Anyone who's trying and risking is going to have some failures amid the successes. Be a good sport about losing. Besides, if you only learn one thing from each bad experience, you're never the loser. But be an even more magnanimous winner. Be humble, never gloating. Give credit where it's due. And remember how phenomenal it feels, so you can do it again!

Leadership. May others be drawn to follow you because they want to go where you're going. May you develop tremendous skills in motivating and inspiring others to accomplish their tasks, to trust in your suggestions. May you engender a team spirit among groups, and be innovative and creative, stepping out in front with superb ideas. Don't be a follower; every time you look side to side, you lose ground. Know who you are and let others seek to be like you. Remember that as you look up to others, others look up to you. Never forget that example is the greatest teacher.

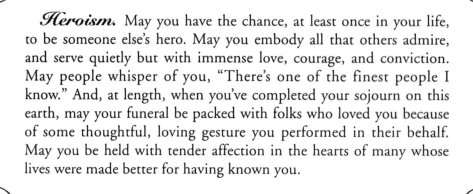

Heroism. May you have the chance, at least once in your life, to be someone else's hero. May you embody all that others admire, and serve quietly but with immense love, courage, and conviction. May people whisper of you, "There's one of the finest people I know." And, at length, when you've completed your sojourn on this earth, may your funeral be packed with folks who loved you because of some thoughtful, loving gesture you performed in their behalf. May you be held with tender affection in the hearts of many whose lives were made better for having known you.

The Right Questions. There's a knack to wondering. For example, if ever you find yourself locked into dealing with a difficult individual, instead of asking, "Why are they like that?" or "How can I accommodate this person?" the right question is, "What is it about me that made me choose/tolerate this?" Instead of thinking, "How would my spouse like me to dress?" the right question is, "How do *I* feel comfortable dressing?" And when tackling a problem, instead of spinning your wheels bemoaning the obvious, seek solutions that move forward. Too many people spend their lives asking all the wrong questions. In every situation may you find the true, core question that matters most.

Quick Responses to Good Ideas. May you never get pulled into a bad decision by an impulsive, knee-jerk reaction, but may you also move quickly enough to seize the moment and take advantage of a great opportunity. Also, never miss the opportunity to soothe another's feelings, and never leave apologies or expressions of love unspoken. Windows of opportunity arise for all of us in which to heal another. Timing is so important. Don't be one who forever looks back with regret at an opportunity missed.

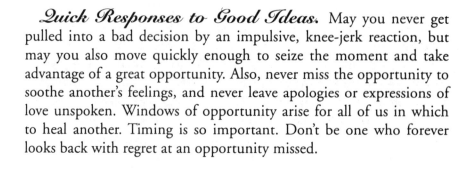

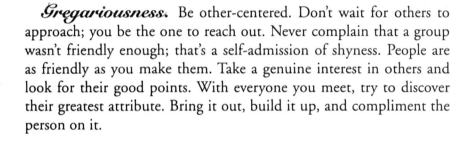

Gregariousness. Be other-centered. Don't wait for others to approach; you be the one to reach out. Never complain that a group wasn't friendly enough; that's a self-admission of shyness. People are as friendly as you make them. Take a genuine interest in others and look for their good points. With everyone you meet, try to discover their greatest attribute. Bring it out, build it up, and compliment the person on it.

Gladness in Others' Triumphs. May you never know a jealous moment, but feel the thrill of a proud parent as you watch others achieve their goals. Share that joy and be grateful for the improvement it brings to your world. Know how valuable you are and swell with that confidence, always acknowledging its source. Then you can be happy for anyone, because the successes of others can never diminish your own.

Altruism. Let the love of your heart widen to include your fellowman, and feel a genuine burning to serve and lift the lives of those around you. Make your most shining moments those times when you help mankind. Have immense compassion, especially with those whose problems you don't understand. Resolve to make the world a better place, then draw up a plan of action. Strive to make your every thought an unselfish one. Your personal happiness will parallel your success.

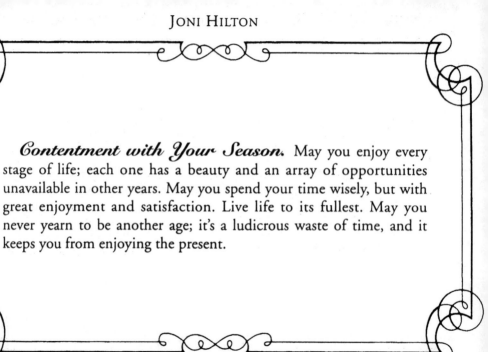

Contentment with Your Season. May you enjoy every stage of life; each one has a beauty and an array of opportunities unavailable in other years. May you spend your time wisely, but with great enjoyment and satisfaction. Live life to its fullest. May you never yearn to be another age; it's a ludicrous waste of time, and it keeps you from enjoying the present.

The Desire to Keep Relationships in Repair. Your relationship with your partner is the Number One relationship; nothing else should come before that. But you should also keep your secondary relationships in good repair, taking time to build memories with people, to be there for them when they need you most, to resolve disagreements and mend breaks as they arise. Don't take friendships for granted; keep a fresh, energetic attitude toward others. Don't just write off someone who's difficult; see it through and work to forgive.

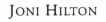

Good Examples. May you be surrounded, through sheer good fortune, by people who set good examples. May they give you hope when you're discouraged, and may you find better ways of living just by watching what they've learned. May your closest associates not only be smart, but wise, and may they share their knowledge with you often. May you know dozens of people who know how to say "I'm sorry," and may you be one who knows how to forgive.

Inner Peace. May you enjoy the placid calm of a clear conscience, the restful heart of one who has served his fellowman, and the warm reassurance of harmony with your God. Forgive those who have wronged you, and release weighty grudges that hold you back. Seek forgiveness from all you could possibly have offended, and let all you love know it.

A Long Life. May every year bring you astonishing lessons to learn, natural beauties to enjoy, fabulous people to love, and rewarding work to do. May each year unfold before you as a colorful palette filled with possibilities. And may you paint your masterpiece with gratitude for every minute you are granted upon this earth.

Honey *on* Hot Bread

and Other Heartfelt Wishes

BY JONI HILTON

A Warm, Wise, and Witty Bundle of Loving Thoughts

Think of your best friend, your spouse, your mother, your child…if you were handing out blessings, what would you wish for each of these loved ones?

Author Joni Hilton has put your fondest wishes into words. Her collection of heartfelt wishes for the important people in your life is a joyful reflection of the familiar hopes and dreams we all share for those we love. *Honey on Hot Bread* is a thoughtful, inspiring book designed to be given to the special person in your life—with love!

50795

ISBN 1-57734-096-5   USA $7.95

9 781577 340966

Covenant
Communications, Inc.